OPEN YOUR HYMNAL *Again*

*More Devotions
That Harmonize
Scripture with Song*

By Denise K. Loock

Open Your Hymnal Again
More Devotions That Harmonize Scripture with Song
By Denise K. Loock

ISBN-978-0-9847655-7-7

Published by Lighthouse Publishing of the Carolinas
2333 Barton Oaks Dr., Raleigh, NC, 27614

Praise for *Open Your Hymnal Again:*

"I've often been told 'you have a song for everything' and it's true that many situations take me back to the hymns and gospel songs that have been stored in my lifetime of music making. That's why I love Denise's *Open Your Hymnal* devotionals and now *Open Your Hymnal Again.* She gives practical biblical devotional truths enhanced with hymn excerpts that clarify those truths. I love the rest and reflect pages that are included in *Open Your Hymnal Again* since I'm one who journals and this gives me opportunity to take the truths presented and apply them to my own life. I'm sure other hymn lovers will be as enthused about it as I am!"

Kathy Benjamin
Musician and Conference Speaker

"With cultural and linguistic insight, with painstaking accountability to the original authors, and with the warmth of heart of a woman of deep faith, Denise Loock once again invites us to open our hymnals. This devotional is a great meditative read for anyone interested in delving deeper into the finest works of our traditional Western hymnody, and offers all of us an opportunity to open our minds, hearts, and ears to the timeless truths of the Gospel pronounced in a historic treasury of artistic beauty."

Rev. David Alexander, ThM, DMin
Staff Chaplain, United States Naval Academy

"Using common objects from our everyday lives, Denise Loock gets her reader to look deeper at their meaning. Then she directs our thoughts to God and gives an insightful correlation. As a final touch—she introduces a hymn that illustrates the truth that was presented. The reader is immediately drawn into the lesson and ends up contemplating how it pertains to his/her own life."

Phyllis Dolislager
Author, *Lessons Learned on the Farm*

Praise for *Open Your Hymnal:*

"a unique collection of devotions that will touch your heart"

Kathleen Hayes
Former editor *The Secret Place*

"You will find the timeless truths expressed in these meditations an encouragement and blessing to your soul."

Mark Hahn
Minister of Music
Belle Mead, NJ

"powerfully relates Scripture, hymns, and biblical knowledge to everyday life"

Jane Carrier Allen
Minister of Worship
Sneads Ferry, NC

"Thanks, Denise, for shedding new light on songs so near to the hearts of people of faith."

Dave and Cheryl Ellington
Worship Leaders
Covington, KY

"These devotions have poured into my soul a deep love for the God we serve."

Connie Cartisano
Author, *Image of the Invisible*

"*Open Your Hymnal* is an excellent resource for pastors . . . a source of great comfort on hospital visits."

Pastor Dave
Sunderland, UK

"a treasure that will inspire you to dig deep into the meaning of each hymn and writer"

Patricia Spies
Women's Ministries
Whiting, NJ

Dedication

To the members of the
Hawk Point Christian Writers' Group—
critics, cheerleaders, colleagues.
Thanks for embracing me as a sister in Christ
and for guiding me as a writer.

As iron sharpens iron,
so a friend sharpens a friend.
Proverbs 27:17 NLT

Author's Note

As you read the meditations in this book, I encourage you to open a hymnal and meditate on the lyrics of the songs that are mentioned. You can also find the lyrics to hundreds of songs and hymns online. The most comprehensive site is cyberhymnal.org. You may also want to explore songsandhymns.org and hymnsite.com.

All the hymn lyrics cited in this book are considered to be in the public domain. Many of them were taken from *Hymns for the Family of God* (Fred Bock, General Editor. Nashville: Paragon Associates, Inc., 1976). Some were taken from cyberhymnal.org, a website which includes many stanzas of the classic hymns that are not typically included in hymnals. The lyrics of "A Christmas Carol" were taken from a reprinted edition of one of Phillips Brooks' hymnals.

Hymnal and website editors sometimes alter both the lyrics and the punctuation of hymns. Occasionally they change the titles. Therefore, the lyrics, titles, and punctuation of hymns in this book may differ from those in the hymnal or website you consult.

Table of Contents

Foreword

One of my favorite snapshots shows what every Christian needs as we grow in faith. An elderly Korean man, on his way to church, carries a book under each arm—one is a Bible and the other a hymnal.

Denise Loock's books, *Open Your Hymnal* and *Open Your Hymnal Again*, combine aspects of the Bible and a hymnal in a fascinating way. Written with great insight, she has created sweet memories of favorite hymns. Specific Scriptures highlight the purpose of each hymn and sometimes added information gives the reason the lyricist wrote the words. I was delighted to find several hymn stories which were new to me.

Denise shares unique events in her life that were touched by a particular Scripture and hymn. She has a way of bringing a tear to the eye or a chuckle to the heart because it is easy to identify with her illustrations.

These 31 selections can fill a month of daily devotionals in a meaningful way. However, once you begin *Open Your Hymnal Again*, it will not be easy to stop reading and wait until the following day to continue. From the opening Scripture passage until the closing Rest and Reflect abundant blessings will enrich the hearts and souls of those who yearn to grow in faith.

Lucy N. Adams
Author, *52 Hymn Story Devotions*
www.52hymns.com

My Spiritual Recliner

I hesitate to admit it, but sometimes the best part of my day is the moment I plop down in my recliner at night. As my body relaxes into the contours of that chair, I feel the stress of the day unraveling. My eyes close and I relish the tranquility.

Resting in the recliner doesn't solve my problems or eliminate my responsibilities. It does, however, provide an oasis of refreshment that enables me to gain some perspective on my circumstances and my concerns. As I sit there, I'm reminded of the blessings of a warm home and a full refrigerator. More importantly, I reflect on the privilege of knowing the one true God who cares about me and who can handle whatever difficulties I encounter.

My end-of-the-day recliner rest is a good example of what Jesus promised us in Matthew

Come to me, all you who are weary and burdened, and I will give you rest.
Matthew 11:28

15

11:28. The Greek word translated "rest" refers to temporary inactivity. For example, it described soldiers who stopped to rest in the midst of an arduous march. If the soldiers hadn't been given this respite, they would've eventually collapsed from exhaustion and been unable to fight.

Resting in my recliner each night rejuvenates my physical body and gives me strength to get up again and do what I need to do. Likewise, resting my spirit in the recliner of God's presence and His promises provides the spiritual strength I need to get up and do the spiritual work God has called me to do—obey His commands and live in a way that brings Him glory.

I wouldn't derive much enjoyment from sitting in my recliner if I kept my back and legs rigid, refusing to trust the support of the chair. Or what if I gripped the arms of the chair tightly as if I were riding a roller coaster? The chair's ability to provide rest for me is directly proportionate to my willingness to trust it.

Methodist minister John Hart Stockton expressed a similar thought in "Only Trust Him." An active evangelist, he wrote the hymn as an invitation to those who hadn't yet accepted Christ as their Savior. However, the lyrics are applicable to Christians too. We need to be reminded that the One who is powerful enough to give us eternal life is also the One who empowers us to live each day as He wants us to live:

Come, every soul by sin oppressed,
There's mercy with the Lord;
And He will surely give you rest
By trusting in His word.

Yes, Jesus is the Truth, the Way,
That leads you into rest;
Believe in Him without delay,
And you'll be fully blessed.

Do we take time each day to rest in our spiritual recliner? To relax in the contours of God's unchanging character and prop up our aching faith on His promises? If we do, those moments will soon become the best part of our day.

Rest and Reflect

How did God restore Elijah's spiritual and physical strength in 1 Kings 19:1–21? How does He restore yours?

Always Rejoice?

Rejoice in the Lord always. I will say it again: Rejoice!
Philippians 4:4

The word *good* has 58 definitions and 271 synonyms according to dictionary.com. It can be used as an adjective, an adverb, an interjection, or a noun. Can you imagine a second-language speaker trying to learn all the nuances of *good?*

On the other hand, some words have just one definition, like the word *always*. Its meaning is clear and uncomplicated—"all the time." So when I read Philippians 4:4, there's not much room for confusion about Paul's meaning.

More than twenty years ago, I heard Elisabeth Elliot, missionary and author, speak at a women's conference. I've never forgotten one of her comments: "The Christian life is simple, but it's never easy." Paul's instructions about rejoicing are a perfect illustration of Elliot's point.

21

There's nothing easy about rejoicing when our lives are churning with turmoil or capsized by tragedy. We may be suffering from a terminal illness. Perhaps we've sent a loved one off to war. Maybe we're praying for a family member who has wandered far from the Lord, or we're wondering how to pay the mortgage. These kinds of circumstances can constrict our faith and cause us to squeak, "Always, Lord? Did you really mean always?"

The simple but difficult answer to that question is "Yes, that's exactly what He meant." But how can we possibly obey that command? Paul supplied the answer within the command: we are to rejoice *in the Lord* not necessarily *in the circumstances*.

22

In Matthew 28, Jesus was preparing His followers for the persecution they were going to encounter as His ambassadors after He returned to heaven. He encouraged them with a promise: "And surely I am with you always" (v. 20). His presence would enable them to overcome whatever obstacles they faced.

As we navigate life's dark waters of difficulty and disappointment, we too can rejoice in the continual presence of the Lord. He stands beside us, ready to keep us on course. We can also rejoice in His steadfast, everlasting love (Jeremiah 31:3).

In 2 Corinthians 9:8 Paul said, "And God is able to make *all* grace abound to you, so that in *all* things at *all* times, having *all* that you need, you will abound in every good work" (emphasis added). These colossal *all*'s balance the weight of "always rejoice."

Maybe British theologian Edward Plumptre had Paul's words in mind when he wrote "Rejoice, Ye Pure in Heart" in 1865. Its inspiring lyrics, coupled with Arthur Messiter's jubilant music, reflected the celebratory mood of the choir festival for which the song was written. And this exhilarating hymn continues to encourage the hearts of God's people almost 150 years later:

> Go on through life's long path,
> Still chanting as ye go;
> From youth to age, by night and day,
> In gladness and in woe;
> Rejoice, rejoice,
> Rejoice, give thanks and sing.

When we open our hearts to God's grace and allow His sufficiency to flow into our lives, He infuses us with the power to praise Him. We can rejoice in the Lord's presence and His provision because He is the Sovereign King of the Universe. And as King He has both the power and the desire to supply what we need (Philippians 4:19).

Rest and Reflect

What situations squash your joy? Inflate your joy by meditating on Paul's words in Philippians 3:20-21 and 4:12-13. List your reasons for rejoicing below.

25

Are You Near
Enough to Yield?

Throughout the three years of Jesus' earthly ministry, people drew near to Him, but not all who approached Jesus truly wanted Him to draw near to them.

Some of the Pharisees and Sadducees came because their curiosity was aroused. But most of the religious leaders wanted to challenge His authority and discredit His ministry. Vast numbers of common people came to Jesus because they wanted tangible gifts—food or healing. A few wanted vindication, like the young man who demanded, "Tell my brother to divide the inheritance with me" (Luke 12:13).

Even the disciples sometimes came with selfish motives. Peter wanted Jesus' stamp of approval on his brand of forgiveness (Matthew 18:21); James and John desired positions of authority in the

Draw near to God and he will draw near to you.
James 4:8a (NASB)

27

kingdom (Matthew 20:20-22).

Jesus let them all come. He let them all ask. But He didn't draw near to all of them, not in the sense that all human beings need Jesus to draw near to them. What we need is the forgiveness He offers and the new life He has promised to those who give Him their full allegiance. He doesn't bestow those gifts on people who come with hands that are quick to grab and run. He entrusts them to those who draw near with hearts that are ready to yield their lives to Him (Hebrews 10:22).

Prolific hymn writer Fanny Crosby approached Jesus with that kind of heart. She knew the difference between drawing near just to take and drawing near to yield. In "I Am Thine, O Lord," she offered this humble prayer:

I am Thine, O Lord, I have heard Thy voice,
And it told Thy love to me;
But I long to rise in the arms of faith,
And be closer drawn to Thee.
Consecrate me now to Thy service, Lord,
By the power of grace divine;
Let my soul look up with a steadfast hope,
And my will be lost in Thine.

It's not wrong to come to Jesus to receive—He tells us to do that so He can give us the help we need (Hebrews 4:16). But He also longs for us to come with empty hands ready to receive His gifts. And He waits for us to give Him the worship He deserves, the gratitude He has earned, and the fellowship He desires.

When we take the time to do that, we will experience the joy Fanny Crosby described in the following way:

O the pure delight of a single hour
That before Thy throne I spend,
When I kneel in prayer, and with Thee, my God,
I commune as friend with friend!

If God seems distant, we need to draw near to Him with hearts that are quick to worship and ready to yield. Then we'll discover that He's been waiting to draw near to us all along.

29

Rest and Reflect

Read Micah 6:6-8. What's the difference between the gifts that please God and those that don't? What specific thing can you do today that will bring Him joy?

_____

_____

_____

_____

_____

_____

_____

_____

_____

_____

_____

_____

_____

_____

_____

_____

_____

_____

_____

_____

_____

_____

_____

_____

_____

The Power
of the Cross

We preach Christ crucified, a stumbling block to the Jews and foolishness to the Gentiles, but to those who God has called, both Jews and Greeks, [it is] the power of God and the wisdom of God.

1 Corinthians 1:23-24

rancis Bacon may have coined the phrase "knowledge is power," but the ancient Greeks were the first to worship at the altar of human intellect. They created words like *philosophia*, the "love of knowledge and wisdom," and *gnosis*, "the special knowledge of spiritual things."

Paul certainly understood how much faith the ancient Greeks put in the power of human wisdom. In his first letter to the Christians of Corinth (a port city on the northeastern coast of Greece), he used the word *power* fifteen times. He wanted the Corinthians to know what was truly powerful and what wasn't.

In chapter 1, Paul used "power of God" twice, and both times he coupled that phrase with Christ's death on the cross (vv. 18, 24). Why is the cross the "power of

33

God"? It is the place where God's holiness triumphed over human sinfulness, where His love and His justice were reconciled. It is the place where redemption was completed, sanctification was born, and eternal life became a reality, not just a dream.

Frederick Whitefield, a 19th century British preacher, expressed the "power of the cross" in "I Saw the Cross of Jesus." The lyrics remind us of the necessity of keeping the cross at the center of our faith:

34

> I saw the cross of Jesus, when burdened with my sin;
> I sought the cross of Jesus, to give me peace within;
> I brought my soul to Jesus,
> He cleansed it in His blood;
> And in the cross of Jesus, I found my peace with God.
>
> I trust the cross of Jesus, in every trying hour,
> My sure and certain refuge, my never failing tower;
> In every fear and conflict, I more than conqueror am;
> Living, I'm safe, or dying,
> Through Christ, the risen Lamb.

The cross is the axis of our salvation—the point at which a holy God can meet unholy people. Both our redemption and our sanctification find their center of gravity there. Christ's work on the cross sealed our adoption as heirs of God and provides the power we need to grow spiritually.

Paul warned the Corinthians that if they diminished the power of the cross by attaching their own wisdom or moral standards to its message, they would "empty the cross of its power" (1:17). He encouraged them to remember what they were like before they heard the message of salvation and to recognize that Christ alone is "wisdom, righteousness, holiness, and redemption" (1:30).

Let's not make the mistake the Corinthians made. Our salvation does not "rest on men's wisdom, but on God's power"—the power of the cross (1 Corinthians 2:5). That is the knowledge that generates true power in our lives.

Rest and Reflect

Read 1 Corinthians 1. In what specific ways has the power of the cross been active in your life recently?

A New Box
of Crayons

And he that sat upon the throne said, "Behold, I make all things new."
Revelation 21:5 (KJV)

Not many experiences gave me more pleasure as a child than opening a new box of crayons. The kaleidoscope of colors, the uniformity of the rows, the perfect points, the waxy smell—I savored that sensory explosion of delight for several moments before I removed the first crayon. Somehow, nothing I created with the crayons ever matched the magic of opening the new box.

I think of that experience when I read Lamentations 3:22-23. Jeremiah said, "Because of the LORD's great love we are not consumed, for his compassions never fail. They are new every morning; great is your faithfulness."

Surprisingly, Jeremiah wrote those confident words during the destruction of Jerusalem. In Lamentations 3, he used graphic phrases to describe the afflictions God had allowed:

39

He has walled me in so I cannot escape;
he has weighed me down with chains.
Even when I call out or cry for help,
he shuts out my prayer.
He has barred my way with blocks of stone;
he has made my paths crooked (v. 7-8).

Jeremiah felt ill-used and discarded—like a broken crayon, its point worn down to the ripped paper casing.

But instead of plummeting into despair, he shifted his gaze to heaven and grabbed hold of hope. Why? Jeremiah counted on God's ability to make all things new. He believed that God would restore Jerusalem, redeem His people, and fulfill every promise He'd made.

The Hebrew word translated "compassions" in Lamentations 3:22 signified the intimate bond between a parent and child—including love, pity, grace, and blessing. No matter how dismal life looked, Jeremiah's confidence in God remained firm.

Swedish hymn writer Lina Sandell was twenty-six years old when she witnessed her father's drowning. But like Jeremiah, her faith remained steadfast in sorrow. Shortly after her father's death, she wrote the following words:

Day by day and with each passing moment,
Strength I find to meet my trials here;
Trusting in my Father's wise bestowment,
I've no cause for worry or for fear.
He whose heart is kind beyond all measure
Gives unto each day what he deems best—
Lovingly, its part of pain and pleasure,
Mingling toil with peace and rest.

Every day the Lord Himself is near me
With a special mercy for each hour;
All my cares He fain would bear, and cheer me,
He whose name is Counselor and Power.
The protection of His child and treasure
Is a charge that on Himself He laid;
"As thy days, thy strength shall be in measure,"
This the pledge to me He made.

God has given us that same promise. Every morning
we wake up with a new crayon box of God's compassions.
He bids us to open it, use it, and share it with others. If
some crayons break or the paper casings tear, that's okay.
Tomorrow God will give us a brand new box. Great is
His faithfulness.

Rest and Reflect

What broken crayons are you mourning? Read Lamentations 3:1-33. What promise of renewal in that passage gives you hope?

42

Serving the
LORD of Hosts

The LORD of hosts is with us; the God of Jacob is our refuge. Selah.
Psalm 46:7 (KJV)

"LORD of hosts" is one of the most frequently used names of God in the Old Testament even though it isn't used even once in the Pentateuch. The Hebrew phrase is *Jehovah Sabaoth* and can be translated "Lord of heavenly hosts," "Lord of angel armies," or "LORD Almighty."

Although the name first appears in 1 Samuel 1:3, it probably refers to Joshua's experience on the eve of the battle of Jericho. As he walked alone in the valley, Joshua encountered "a man . . . with a drawn sword in his hand" and asked, "Are you for us or for our enemies?" (Joshua 5:13)

The man replied, "I come now as captain of the host of the Lord" (v. 14, NASB). Joshua's reaction to those words—he fell to the ground in worship—indicates that the "man" who stood before him

45

was God in human form.

Many years later, when David responded to Goliath's taunts he declared, "I come against you in the name of the LORD of the hosts—*Jehovah Sabaoth*—God of the armies of Israel" (1 Samuel 17:45). Maybe David believed that the heavenly hosts of God's angels would swoop down upon the valley of Elah and destroy the Philistines as they had defeated the Canaanites in the past (see Exodus 23:20-23). Maybe he counted on some other supernatural intervention—hailstones (Joshua 10:11) or panic (1 Samuel 14:15).

The point is that David knew he didn't have to fight Goliath alone. He was certain that *Jehovah Sabaoth* would defend His honor and His people. In confidence David proclaimed, "The battle is the LORD's, and he will give you into our hands" (1 Samuel 17: 47).

Martin Luther was embroiled in a different kind of battle when he wrote "A Mighty Fortress Is Our God" in the 1520s. As the leader of the Protestant Reformation, he had been declared Public Enemy Number 1 by the Roman Catholic Church.

According to his biographers, Luther often re-charged his spirit by singing the hymn that has encouraged Christians for almost 500 years:

Did we in our own strength confide,
Our striving would be losing;
Were not the right Man on our side,
The Man of God's own choosing:
Dost ask who that may be?
Christ Jesus it is He;
Lord Sabaoth, His Name,
From age to age the same,
And He must win the battle.

Luther relied on the "LORD of hosts," *Jehovah Sabaoth*, just as Joshua did at Jericho and David did in the Valley of Elah. These men wholeheartedly followed God's directives even though common sense and self-preservation suggested other tactics. And God honored their allegiance with astounding victories.

I don't know what walled cities tower over you this week or what giants threaten to "give your flesh to the birds of the air"(1 Samuel 17:44). But I do know that *Jehovah Sabaoth* is still in the deliverance business. He will win the battle. In confidence all His children can say, "O LORD of Hosts, blessed is the man who trusts in you (Psalm 84:12 KJV).

47

Rest and Reflect

Read David's conversation with Goliath with a fresh perspective (1 Samuel 17: 41-47). What was David's goal in verse 46-47? What is your goal today?

_____

_____

_____

_____

_____

_____

_____

_____

_____

_____

_____

_____

_____

_____

_____

_____

_____

_____

_____

_____

_____

_____

_____

_____

_____

_____

_____

_____

_____

_____

_____

_____

_____

_____

_____

_____

_____

_____

_____

_____

_____

The Book for Me

If you attended Sunday school as a child, you probably learned this simple song:

> The B-I-B-L-E
> Yes, that's the book for me.
> I stand alone
> On the Word of God,
> The B-I-B-L-E.

Your laws are my treasure; they are my heart's delight.
Psalm 119:111 (NLT)

But is the Bible truly "the book" for you? It was for David. He wrote all 176 verses of Psalm 119 to explain why the Bible was "the book" for him.

David declared repeatedly that the law of God was his "delight." That's especially interesting when we realize that in David's time the law of God was comprised of the first seven books of our Bible—Genesis through Judges.

"Really, David?" I want to ask. Maybe Genesis, along with parts of Exodus and

51

Joshua. But Leviticus and all its rules? Judges and all its failures? Yet David fervently declared, "Oh, how I love thy law" (v. 97).

David viewed the Scriptures as Indiana Jones viewed the hunt for a lost artifact. Nothing prevented him from seeking it: "I rejoice in your promise like one who finds great spoil," David wrote (v. 162). What priceless gems did he discover? He found counsel, strength, freedom, comfort, wisdom, joy, and peace (v. 24, 28, 32, 52, 98, 111, 165).

David prayed, "Open my eyes that I may see wonderful things in your law" (v. 18). The Hebrew word for "open," *galah*, literally means "to uncover" or "to remove." It described a woman unveiling her face. It also referred to uncovering one's ear by pushing aside the hair as if you were about to tell someone a secret.

David prayed that God would tell him some secrets—reveal to him what a casual observer or listener couldn't detect. David's desire involved more than a simple understanding of the words; he wanted to understand the God who had spoken the words—His character, His ways, His desires.

David recognized that the only way to gain that depth of discernment was by meditating on God's Word. The Hebrew word for "meditate" means "to speak with oneself, murmuring in a low voice." It's a conscious, repeated act, one we practice when we're trying to digest the full meaning of a statement—the nuances of a love letter or the intricacies of a mathematical equation.

John Burton, Sr., was an English layman who taught children in his church and wrote Sunday school materials and songs. He published at least three volumes of hymns for children. The most well-known of his songs is "Holy Bible, Book Divine":

Holy Bible, book divine,
Precious treasure, thou art mine:
Mine to tell me whence I came;
Mine to teach me which I am.

Mine to comfort in distress,
Suffering in this wilderness;
Mine to show, by living faith,
Man can triumph over death.

53

Burton believed that a love for God's Word would provide an indestructible foundation for the children he taught. It works for adults, too. If we ask God to open our eyes to the dazzling wonders of His Word, we'll discover the priceless treasures within its pages. And we'll testify, as David did, "Your law is my delight" (v. 77).

Rest and Reflect

Make a list of the benefits of meditating on God's Word that are given in Psalm 119.

54

_____

_____

_____

_____

_____

_____

_____

_____

_____

_____

_____

_____

_____

_____

_____

_____

_____

What's Perched
in Your Soul?

Which Old Testament character had the most to say about hope? Job did. Surprised? Me, too—at first. But the more I thought about it, the more I realized that the most natural thing for Job to do, from a spiritual perspective, was to nurture hope. Instead of Job's name being synonymous with suffering, maybe we should link his name with hope.

Where then is my hope? Who can see any hope for me?
Job 17:15

American poet Emily Dickinson wrote, "Hope is the thing with feathers / That perches in the soul, / And sings the tune—without the words, / And never stops at all." Whenever I read her description of hope, I think of Job. Because hope was perched in his soul, he sang faith's tune while everyone around him chanted a dirge of doom.

How did Job do that? Hope maintained its grip in his soul because it was perched on Job's

57

intimate knowledge of God. Job was righteous; he "feared God and shunned evil" (Job 1:1). Therefore, even as he mourned the death of all his children, the destruction of all his crops and livestock, and scraped his sores with pottery fragments, Job testified, "After my skin has been destroyed, yet in my flesh I will see God" (19:26).

Job didn't develop that kind of character on his own—those qualities grew in him because he cultivated a personal relationship with God. He declared, "I have not departed from the commands of his lips; I have treasured the words of his mouth more than my daily bread" (23:12).

However, keeping hope in his heart wasn't easy. Job 13:15 is often translated "Though he slay me, I will hope in him." But the Hebrew wording in that verse could be rendered, "Behold, he will slay me; I have no hope" (alternate translation in ESV). Other verses also reveal Job's internal battle: "What strength do I have, that I should still hope?" (6:11) and "My days are swifter than a weaver's shuttle, and they come to an end without hope" (7:6).

Nevertheless, Job didn't allow the hawk of despair to drive away the songbird of hope. In chapter 14 he declared, "All the days of my hard service I will wait for my renewal to come" (v. 14).

That confidence in eternal life is the reason Job didn't follow his wife's advice to "curse God and die" (2:9). Hope triumphed because Job believed that suffering on earth would yield incomparable blessings in heaven: "When he has tested me, I will come forth as gold" (23:10).

German-born Joachim Neander wrote "All My Hope on God Is Founded" almost 400 years ago. Like Job, he realized that possessions, power, and achievements often crumbled. Only hope endured:

> All my hope on God is founded;
> He doth still my trust renew,
> Me through change and chance He guideth,
> Only good and only true.
> God unknown, He alone
> Calls my heart to be His own.

59

> Pride of man and earthly glory,
> Sword and crown betray his trust;
> What with care and toil he buildeth,
> Tower and temple fall to dust.
> But God's power, hour by hour,
> Is my temple and my tower.

God gives each of us the opportunity to know Him intimately and to trust Him confidently whether we receive trophies or troubles from His hand. Can we, like Job and Neander, sing faith's tune "without the words and never [stop] at all"? That depends on what's perched in our souls.

Rest and Reflect

God may never answer some questions that we ask. How does faith respond to those unanswered questions? Read Job 42:1-6 and Romans 11:33-36.

No Condemnation

...So we too have put our faith in Christ Jesus that we may be justified by faith in Christ and not by observing the law, because by observing the law no one will be justified.
Galatians 2:16

harles Wesley grew up in a preacher's home. His mother included daily Bible readings and Scripture memorization in the educational routine of her children. At age eight, Charles was sent to live with his older brother Samuel, who supervised his younger brother's religious and academic education until Charles enrolled at Oxford University.

As a student at Oxford, Charles developed a rigid regimen of Bible study, prayer, and charitable activities. He even went to America as a missionary. But neither his spiritual disciplines nor his good works provided the peace he sought. He still felt chained by his sinfulness and unworthy of God's love. At age thirty-one he was incapacitated by an extended illness. During his recovery, he read Martin Luther's commentary on

63

Galatians and learned what justification by faith alone meant.

The Greek word for "justified" means "to declare, to pronounce righteous." It doesn't mean "just as if I never sinned." As Thayer's Lexicon says, it "never means to *make* worthy, but to *judge* worthy or *treat* worthy."

The whole point of justification is that nothing we ever did or could do makes us worthy of salvation. The weight of our sin (past, present, and future) will forever prevent us from balancing God's scales of justice. He has pardoned us only because Christ died in our place. His death didn't erase our sins; the magnitude of His sacrifice balanced the scales of God's justice. And once those scales were balanced, nothing can ever unbalance them again.

When Charles Wesley realized this truth, he was overjoyed. He expressed that joy in a hymn—"And Can It Be That I Should Gain," which was initially published under the title "Free Grace." The hymn's autobiographical tone is established through Wesley's use of first person pronouns—*I, me, my,* and *mine.* In stanza 5 he used "I feel" twice, emphasizing the peace and certainty that filled his soul:

> Still the small inward voice I hear,
> That whispers all my sins forgiven;
> Still the atoning blood is near,
> That quenched the wrath of hostile Heaven.

I feel the life His wounds impart;
I feel the Savior in my heart.

Stanza 6 is Wesley's shout of elation:

No condemnation now I dread;
Jesus, and all in Him, is mine;
Alive in Him, my living Head,
And clothed in righteousness divine,
Bold I approach th'eternal throne,
And claim the crown, through Christ my own.

The fact that our salvation depends on Christ alone should fill our hearts with peace and joy, too. I've sung Wesley's words many times: "Amazing Love! How can it be that thou, my God shoulds't die for me?" Am I truly amazed by the magnitude of His sacrifice? If so, does my life radiate the joy and peace that "no condemnation" imparts?

*biographical information on Wesley summarized from *Assist Me to Proclaim: The Life and Hymns of Charles Wesley* by John R. Tyson, Eerdmans, 2007.

Rest and Reflect

Read Galatians 3 this week. What does the phrase "belong to Christ" in verse 29 signify to you? Do you understand why this portion of Scripture filled Wesley with joy?

_____

_____

_____

_____

_____

_____

_____

_____

_____

_____

_____

_____

_____ 67

_____

_____

_____

_____

_____

_____

_____

_____

_____

_____

_____

_____

The Miracle
in the Mirror

The English word *miracle* comes from a Latin word, *miraculum*, which means "object of wonder." In the Bible, the word *miracle* is always used in reference to a marvelous demonstration of God's power.

We normally use *miracle* to describe physical acts of God's power such as Moses parting the Red Sea and Jesus raising Lazarus from the dead. However, the most amazing demonstration of God's power occurs when He transforms us into living sanctuaries.

Think about it. In the Old Testament God's presence dwelled in the tabernacle's Holy of Holies. Its walls and floor were overlaid with pure gold. Its ceiling an intricately woven tapestry of scarlet, white, indigo, and gold threads. The only object in the room was the Ark of the Covenant, also overlaid with pure gold and adorned with

Let us purify ourselves from everything that contaminates body and spirit, perfecting holiness out of reverence for God.

2 Corinthians 7:1

69

Denise K. Loock

cherubim hammered out of solid blocks of gold. The dazzling beauty of this room was an appropriate place for a holy God to dwell.

But now He lives in us. In *us*. Our bodies are a conglomeration of dying cells, disobedient wills, and sinful urges. Nevertheless, we've become objects of wonder because God in His mercy has chosen to make our hearts His dwelling place.

No wonder Paul urged the Corinthians to keep themselves pure and admonished them with these words: "Do you not know that your body is a temple of the Holy Spirit?" (1 Corinthians 6:19). Paul had never seen the original Holy of Holies that Moses had constructed; neither could he have entered the Holy of Holies that existed in his day. Only one person was allowed to enter that sacred room—the High Priest once a year on the Day of Atonement. That's how separate God was from His sinful children, and that's how serious He was about protecting the purity of His dwelling.

How could God exchange the splendor and purity of the Holy of Holies for the dilapidated shack of a human body? Two reasons. First, He loves us. Secondly, when He looks at us, He sees perfection and beauty because we have been made holy through Christ's redemptive work on the cross (Hebrews 10:10, 14). That's the miracle of mercy we see in the mirror every day.

You may not have looked at yourself as an object of wonder lately, but that's exactly what each of us is. We don't have walls of gold or sparkling cherubim, but we are the temple in which God chooses to dwell.

Paul told the Corinthians to "honor God with your body" (1 Corinthians 6:20). How can we do that? Frances R. Havergal, a British hymn writer and author, suggested the following method in one of her best-known hymns:

Take my life and let it be
Consecrated, Lord, to Thee;
Take my hands and let them move
At the impulse of Thy love.

Take my feet and let them be
Swift and beautiful for Thee:
Take my voice and let me sing
Always, only for my King.

Take my love, my God, I pour
At Thy feet its treasures store;
Take myself and I will be
Ever only, all for Thee.

In her devotional classic *Kept for the Master's Use* Havergal wrote, "Having already said, 'Take my life,' let us now say, with deepened conviction, 'Keep my life, for I cannot keep it for Thee.'"* Jesus is the only one who could transform our lives into miracles of mercy—appropriate homes for His presence. He's also the only one who can keep our living tabernacles clean. Allowing Him the freedom to scrub the impurities out of our lives is the best way to honor Him. That should prompt each of us to ask, how clean is my temple?

Kept for the Master's Use by Frances Ridley Havergal. James Nisbet and Co., 1881, p.14

Rest and Reflect

In 1 Corinthians 6:12 Paul wrote, "Everything is permissible for me, but not everything is beneficial." Are there some non-beneficial behaviors or habits that Jesus needs to sweep out of your temple?

73

Thanksgiving Fireworks

Give thanks to the LORD for he is good; for his steadfast love endures forever.
Psalm 136:1 (ESV)

"Nobody should ever read Shakespeare's plays," I used to tell my high school English students. Then I'd wait for the disbelief to spread across their faces. Their widened eyes and wrinkled foreheads revealed their puzzlement: Our English teacher doesn't want us to read Shakespeare?

After a long pause I'd add, "To fully appreciate his genius, his plays must be experienced—professional actors performing on stage with minimal props and maximum passion. *That's* Shakespeare. Anything less is like watching fireworks on a 12" black and white TV."

I feel the same way about Psalm 136. It loses a tremendous amount of its power when it's confined to a piece of paper. In Old Testament times it was part of corporate worship, read at Passover and other festivals.

75

The hundreds of worshipers who gathered in the temple's courtyard recited the psalm responsively. The worship leader proclaimed each verse's affirmation of God's goodness. Then the crowd's refrain of "for his steadfast love endures forever" echoed across the courtyard, an orchestra of human voices.

Psalm 136 begins with a declaration of who God is. He is LORD (*Yahweh*), the great I AM, the covenant-keeping redeemer of Israel. He is God of gods (*Elohim*), the creator and sustainer of the world. He is Lord of lords (*Adonai*), Israel's owner, protector, and master.

Verses 4-9 highlight God's goodness manifested in creation. Its beauty, order, and efficiency continually display His generosity to every human being. Then verses 10-22 proclaim God's goodness to Israel—deliverance from Egypt's bondage, guidance through the wilderness, and the provision of a land inheritance.

The final verses praise the One who continues to recognize His people's neediness and gives "food to every creature" (verse 25). And then with a deafening roar the crowd shouted out the finale: "Give thanks to the God of heaven, for his steadfast love endures forever" (v. 26, ESV).

August Ludvig Storm also used a repetitive format when he wrote "Thanks to God for My Redeemer." In the three stanzas of his hymn, he listed twenty-four reasons to give thanks. Like the psalmist, he referred to both physical and spiritual blessings:

Thanks to God for my Redeemer,
Thanks for all Thou dost provide!
Thanks for times now but a memory,
Thanks for Jesus by my side!
Thanks for pleasant, balmy springtime,
Thanks for dark and dreary fall!
Thanks for tears by now forgotten,
Thanks for peace within my soul!

When I reflect on Storm's lyrics, gratitude swells in my heart just as Israel's praises surge in Psalm 136. His words also remind me to be thankful for small blessings like "roses by the wayside" and vast ones like "grace that none can measure."

When you gather with your loved ones at Thanksgiving, suggest a reading of Psalm 136 or Storm's hymn. Perhaps your family would like to create its own hymn. Both the psalmist's and Storm's patterns are easy to follow.

Your family's hymn may not be as spectacular as live theatre or Fourth of July fireworks, but God won't be disappointed. He always appreciates a radiant display of praise.

Rest and Reflect

What evidence of God's steadfast love have you seen recently? What "roses by the wayside" has He provided for you? List at least five.

_____

_____

_____

_____

_____

_____

_____

_____

_____

_____

_____

_____

_____

_____

_____

_____

_____

_____

_____

_____

_____

_____

The LORD
Is Coming Again

The somber church music of the 18th century frustrated Isaac Watts. Most congregations in his era only sang the psalms. John Calvin had said, "God had provided his people with a set of inspired hymns in Holy Scripture" and concluded that no other words should be used in worship services. Watts, however, wanted to use lyrics that were more understandable and tunes that were more uplifting.

Watts attempted to update church music by paraphrasing all 150 psalms in lyrical English rhymed verse. Several of the hymns that we sing today first appeared in his book, *The Psalms of David*— "Jesus Shall Reign Where'er the Sun" (Psalm 72), "O God Our Help in Ages Past"(Psalm 90), and "Joy to the World" (Psalm 98).

"Joy to the World" is one of the most popular Christmas

The LORD has made his salvation known and revealed his righteousness to the nations.
Psalm 98:2

81

carols in the English-speaking world. However, a close examination of Psalm 98 reveals that this favorite advent hymn refers to much more than the birth of Christ. In fact, it is primarily a celebration of His future role as King of Kings.

The first few verses of the psalm can certainly be applied to Christ's birth. God did make "his salvation known and revealed his righteousness" when Jesus was born in Bethlehem (v. 2). And His love and faithfulness to Israel was manifested through the arrival of their Messiah (v. 3).

However, throughout Psalm 98 the psalmist also referred to events that haven't occurred. For example, in verse 3 he said, "All the ends of the earth have seen the salvation of our God." When will that be accomplished? Verse 9 tells us—when "he will judge the world in righteousness and the peoples with equity." That is the day Paul spoke of when he wrote that every knee will bow and every tongue confess that Jesus Christ is LORD (Philippians 2:10). That didn't happen when Jesus came to earth as a baby; it will happen when He returns as King.

Watts certainly understood that Psalm 98 referred primarily to the second coming of Christ. References to Christ's future kingdom are woven into every stanza. When will "rocks, hills, and plains repeat the sounding joy"? When will "heaven and nature sing"? Paul said that all of creation waits for the day when Christ will return to earth as king (Romans 8:19-23).

When will sin and sorrow no longer grow or "thorns infest the ground"? When will Jesus come "to make His blessings flow far as the curse is found"? Revelation 21:1 tells us that time will come when "the first heaven and the first earth had passed away."

Is it inappropriate to sing "Joy to the World" at Christmastime? Of course not. But its joyful message shouldn't be confined to the advent season. Every day our desire should be "let earth receive her King" as we eagerly anticipate Jesus' return. Every day our prayer should be "let every heart prepare Him room." And every day the joyful message of our lives should be:

83

> He rules the world with truth and grace,
> And makes the nations prove
> The glories of His righteousness
> And wonders of His love.

Rest and Reflect

Isaiah 11:1-9 and 60:1-22 describe Christ's kingdom. Read these passages and rejoice over the future blessings that we will enjoy.

_____

_____

_____

_____

_____

_____

_____

_____

_____

_____

_____

85

_____

_____

_____

_____

_____

_____

_____

_____

_____

_____

_____

_____

_____

The Everlasting Light of Christmas

I have come into the world as a light, so that no one who believes in me should stay in darkness.

John 12:46

For Americans, 1865 was a bittersweet year. On April 9, Lee surrendered to Grant at the Appomattox Courthouse, staunching the torrent of blood that flowed from the veins of our nation during the Civil War. But just five days later, John Wilkes Booth assassinated President Lincoln. The wounds inflicted by both the war and the murder impaired the nation's health for decades.

It was a bittersweet year for Phillips Brooks, too. An ardent abolitionist, the Philadelphia clergyman rejoiced over the Emancipation Proclamation. However, he continued to work on behalf of the freed slaves, recognizing that their physical liberation hadn't given them the civil freedoms they deserved as citizens. The severity of the country's spiritual and political condition still troubled him.

Late in 1865 Brooks traveled to the Holy Land. On Christmas Eve "he rode on horseback from Jerusalem to Bethlehem. And as twilight was falling, he went out to the field where tradition says the shepherds saw the glory of the LORD."* The stillness of the night and the splendor of the stars soothed his anxious soul, and his heart swelled with hope.

Two years later, the serenity of that Judean panorama inspired Brooks to write a song for the children of his church to sing on Christmas morning. "O Little Town of Bethlehem" celebrates the glorious truth that "in this world of sin" the gift of salvation provides hope for all:

88

Where children pure and happy
Pray to the blessed Child
Where misery cries out to Thee,
Son of the Mother mild;
Where charity stands watching
And Faith hold wide the door,
The dark night wakes, the glory breaks,
And Christmas comes once more.

Brooks devoted his life to sharing that message of hope with others. He knew that the love of God was the remedy for everything that afflicted his congregation and his country. In another song, "A Christmas Carol," Brooks wrote:

Then let every heart keep its Christmas within,
Christ's pity for sorrow, Christ's hatred for sin,
Christ's care for the weakest, Christ's courage for right,
Christ's dread of the darkness, Christ's love of the light.**

Like Brooks we live in a world filled with suffering, sorrow, and injustice. This may have been a bittersweet year for you and your loved ones. Don't allow disappointment to overwhelm you. The Everlasting Light still shines, and God still "imparts to human hearts the blessings of His heav'n." As long as His Light shines in our hearts, darkness cannot defeat us.

Al Smith's Treasury of Hymn Histories by Alfred B. Smith. Special Library Edition. Heritage Music Distributors, Inc., 1982.
**Christmas Songs and Easter Carols* by Phillips Brooks. E. P. Dutton and Co., 1903. Reprint edition. Kessinger Publishing Rare Prints, 2010.

Rest and Reflect

Compare Jesus' words in John 12:44–46 with David's words in Psalm 119:105 and Solomon's in Proverbs 6:20-23. How is it possible for us to continually bask in the everlasting light Jesus provides?

90

91

Why So Merry,
Gentlemen?

*Comfort,
comfort my people,
says your God...the
glory of the Lord will be
revealed and all mankind
together will see it...*

Isaiah 40:1, 5

We sang a lot of Christmas carols in the church I attended as a child, but we never sang "God Rest Ye Merry, Gentlemen." Sometimes I wonder if our choir director just didn't know what "rest you merry" meant and didn't want to generate questions from inquisitive children that he couldn't answer.

"God Rest Ye Merry, Gentlemen" is one of the oldest Christmas carols we have. According to several sources, its lyrics date back to the fifteenth century. The song first appeared in print in the 1833 edition of William B. Sandys' *Christmas Carols Ancient and Modern*, which also included "The First Noel."

No one knows who wrote the carol's seven verses, but the writer definitely understood the significance of Christ's birth. Twice he reminded us

93

that Christ our Savior was born to free us from "Satan's power." He also made it clear that our Savior is the Son of God.

Other than its odd title, the most familiar part of the carol is its refrain: "O tidings of comfort and joy." We usually define the noun *comfort* as "a person or thing that brings relief." But in the fifteenth century, the word had a slightly different meaning. It comes from an Old French word that literally means "with strength." It referred to both mental and physical strength.

The hymn writer used *comfort* because he was talking about the source of the strength that saved us from Satan's power. The answer of course is Jesus Christ. As the fourth stanza states:

94

"Fear not, then" said the angel,
"Let nothing you afright.
This day is born a Savior
 Of a pure Virgin bright,
 To free all those who trust in Him
 From Satan's power and might.

Paul made that same point in Romans 7. He was agonizing over his inability to conquer sin: "For I have the desire to do what is good, but I cannot carry it out. For what I do is not the good I want to do; no, the evil I do not want to do, this I keep on doing" (vv. 18-19). In frustration he cried out, "What a wretched man I am! Who will rescue me from this body of death?" (v. 24). And then with great joy he gives the answer: "Thanks be to God—through Jesus Christ our Lord" (v. 25).

This profound truth is the message of "comfort and joy" that the angels brought to the shepherds and everyone else. It's also the theme of "God Rest Ye Merry, Gentlemen." The archaic phrase "rest ye merry" means "rest assured," so the phrase "God rest you merry" can be paraphrased "may God keep you assured" or "may God keep you confident."

In other words, the carol's writer is saying, "There's no need to be afraid, fellow Christian, about your standing with God. And do not be discouraged as you battle sin in your daily walk of faith. God provided a Savior who freed you from Satan's power. That Savior also gives you the strength to triumph over your sinful nature." That's a message of "comfort and joy" that should keep our hearts singing all year long.

95

Rest and Reflect

Read Romans 7:14-8:3. Why should these affirmations fill our hearts with "comfort and joy"?

Grace Greater
Than Our Sin

The grace of our Lord was poured out on me abundantly, along with the faith and love that are in Christ Jesus.
1 Timothy 1:14

o you remember using the phrase "very, very" as a child to describe the magnitude of something? A "very, very big" dog, perhaps? Or at the conclusion of a school essay did you ever write, "the very, very end"?

I used the phrase often until one of my teachers declared war on my *very* habit. "One *very* is enough," she wrote on my papers and drew blood red lines through the extra ones. After that, I stopped including the extra *very's* in my stories, but mentally I still used them. In certain situations, two *very's* just seemed necessary—"I love you very, very much."

Paul used a Greek version of "very, very" in 1 Timothy 1:14. He was reflecting on his life before Jesus confronted him on the road to Damascus. Paul said, "I was once a blasphemer and a persecutor and a violent man" (v. 13). But he added, "the

99

grace of our Lord was poured out on me abundantly" (v. 14). In Greek "abundantly" is *hyperpleonazo*, which literally means "abundantly abundant." That's the reason the KJV uses "exceeding abundant" and the ASV uses "abounded exceedingly" in this verse. For Paul, one *abundant* just wasn't enough to describe the grace that God had poured out on him, the self-acknowledged "chief of sinners" (v. 15).

Julia Harriet Johnston also understood the "very, very" aspect of God's grace. She wrote the lyrics to "Grace Greater Than Our Sin." However, her life story was nothing like Paul's. In fact, I doubt that anyone ever used the words *blasphemer, persecutor,* or *violent* in reference to her.

She was raised in a Christian home and headed the Sunday school department in her church for 40 years. She also served as the president of the local chapter of the Presbyterian Missionary Society and wrote over 500 hymns. But just like you and me, Julia Johnston still needed God's abundantly abundant grace, the grace that "exceeds our sin and our guilt," the grace that "points to the Refuge, the mighty Cross."

Johnston doesn't use "very, very" or "abundantly abundant" in her hymn; she uses her own seemingly redundant phrase: "marvelous, infinite, matchless grace." The repetition of *grace* in the refrain suggests that she too was overwhelmed by the magnitude of the grace that flowed into her life, and that she also had difficulty finding suitable words to express her wonder and her gratitude:

> Grace, grace, God's grace,
> Grace that will pardon and cleanse within;
> Grace, grace, God's grace,
> Grace that is greater than all our sin.

As a child, I used "very, very" because words like *gargantuan* and *delectable* weren't part of my vocabulary. But when it comes to God's grace, no words can describe its immensity or infinity. That's why Paul resorted to redundancy and Johnston to repetition. Which is fine with me. After all, if God's grace was describable, it wouldn't be able to cover my sins and yours. And that's the kind of grace we need. Abundantly abundant, very, very big grace.

Rest and Reflect

Read 1 Timothy 1:12–16. How has God displayed his Grace Greater Than Our Sin in your life? Do you respond to His grace as Paul did in verse 17?

103

The Sunday School
Sand Pile

I will exalt you, my God the King; I will praise your name forever and ever.

Psalm 145:1

nce upon a time a Unitarian minister spoke at a primary school graduation. His simple yet profound content touched many hearts. Eventually his speech was featured in a "Dear Abby" column. Then its popularity increased so rapidly that the minister, Robert Fulghum, added a few more thoughts and turned it into a book—*All I Need to Know I Learned in Kindergarten.* The book became an international phenomenon and made Fulghum a best-selling author.

In that graduation address Fulghum observed, "Wisdom was not at the top of the graduate school mountain, but there in the sand pile at Sunday School."* I'd have to agree with him, for it was in Sunday school that I learned Psalm 100.

I can't remember which of my Sunday school teachers

105

encouraged me to learn the five short verses of this hymn the Israelites sang as they gathered for worship. Neither do I remember what trinket she dangled in front of me as an incentive for memorizing the psalm.

What I do know is that the simple truths of Psalm 100 laid a spiritual foundation for my faith that has withstood the storms of my adult life. So with apologies to Robert Fulghum for borrowing his idea and in honor of his commitment to brevity and simplicity, I offer a companion piece to his well-known words:

All I Need to Know I Learned from Psalm 100
Praise God loud and often.

Do God's work with a happy heart.
Sing in God's presence—don't whine.
There's only one God.
He made me. I belong to him.
He's my shepherd. I need to follow him.
Thank Him and praise Him in church.
Thank Him and praise Him everywhere else, too.
God is good. All the time.
God is loving. All the time.
God is faithful. All the time.

Psalm 100 contains simple phrases that children can memorize easily and profound principles that children understand quickly. It also contains rock-solid truths that no adult problem or doubt can fracture.

Each of its five verses emphasizes the gratitude and gladness that should radiate from our lives as children of God. That in itself is a life-long assignment for me since I tend to be more of a skeptical Scrooge than a perky Pollyanna.

Many hymns are based on Psalm 100. One of them is William Kethe's "All People That on Earth Do Dwell." In it he wrote:

O enter then His gates with praise,
Approach with joy His courts unto;
Praise, laud, and bless His name always,
For it is seemly to do so.

Seemly is an old-fashioned word, but it means "becoming, appropriate, and admirable." Nothing in life is more seemly than praising God. Many of us learned that lesson long ago in Sunday school. And we're still learning it because we'll never outgrow the need to be reminded to praise His name.

All I Really Need to Know I Learned in Kindergarten. Robert Fulghum. Fifteenth Anniversary Edition. New York: Ballantine Books, 2003.

Rest and Reflect

What Scripture passages are foundational to your faith? Take a familiar passage like Psalm 23 or Psalm 91 and rewrite it in your own words.

_____

_____

_____

_____

_____

_____

_____

_____

_____

_____

_____ 109

_____

_____

_____

_____

_____

_____

_____

_____

_____

_____

_____

On What Is Our Gaze
Fixed?

The portraits of many men and women adorn the walls of the Great Hall of Heroes described in Hebrews 11. Two colossal paintings dominate the room—Abraham and Moses. Fourteen of the chapter's forty verses are devoted to these Old Testament VIPs.

What strikes me most about the two men is their capacity to embrace the eternal. Abraham lived in tents after he left Ur because he was "looking forward to the city with foundations, whose architect and builder is God" (v. 10). Moses cast aside all the wealth he enjoyed as the adopted son of Pharaoh's daughter because he was "looking ahead to his reward" (v. 26).

The Greek word translated "looking forward" in verse 10 is *ekdechomai*, which means "expect, wait for." It suggests inevitability, as in someone

Now faith is being sure of what we hope for and certain of what we do not see.

Hebrews 11:1

111

waiting for sunrise. Both Abraham and Moses displayed that kind of confidence in the promises God had given them.

The word translated "looking ahead" in verse 26 is *apoblepo*, which means "to look with steadfast mental gaze." It conveys fixation, as in "nothing is going to keep me from doing this." We might use the phrase "bound and determined."

Plenty of circumstances in Abraham's and Moses' lives could have distracted them. For example, Genesis 21:11 indicates that Abraham was heartbroken when God commanded him to send his son Ishmael away. Moses was equally devastated when God told him he would not enter the Promised Land (Deuteronomy 3:26). Neither man, however, wallowed in self-pity or tumbled into despair. Both of them kept their gaze fixed on their eternal reward.

No one knows who wrote the words to "I Am Bound for the Kingdom," which first appeared in *Family Hymns*, published by the American Tract Society in 1835. But the author displays the same kind of faith that Moses and Abraham had:

Whither goest thou, Pilgrim stranger
Passing thro' this darksome vale?
Know'st thou not 'tis full of danger,
And will not thy courage fail?

Pilgrim thou dost justly call me,
Wandering o'er this waste so wide;
Yet no harm will e'er befall me,
While I'm blessed with such a Guide.

I am bound for the kingdom,
Will you go to glory with me?
Hallelujah, Praise the Lord!

Plenty of challenges in the darksome vale of life threaten to make our courage fail too. But when we fix our mental gaze on our Guide, we can walk with confidence just as the Old Testament saints did. "These were all commended for their faith, yet none of them received what had been promised" (Hebrews 11: 39). They were "bound for glory" with their eyes fixed on what lay ahead. On what is our gaze fixed?

Denise K. Loock

Rest and Reflect

Read more about Moses' faith in Deuteronomy 31:1-8 or Abraham's faith in Romans 4:18-21. On which of God's promises will you focus today?

114

King of All

How awesome is the LORD Most High, the great King over all the earth.

Psalm 47:2

In the spring of 2010, 26-year-old Steve Carse decided to arrange his own coronation. So the unemployed visionary purchased an umbrella cart, parked it on a busy Atlanta corner, and began selling handcrafted popsicles. He crowned himself the King of Pops.

His ingenuity not only solved his financial problems but also brought him celebrity status. He's popular on Twitter® and Facebook®. He's been featured in numerous newspaper articles and also on CNN. Carse is proof that, with perseverance and publicity, almost anyone in America can be crowned king of something.

If you play video games, you can be the King of Swords, the King of Fools, or even the King of Zombies. Thanks to the DIY network, Gino Panaro became the King of Dirt. Many

117

other monarchs rule on the Web: King of Carpets, King of Cars, King of Shaves, King of Pork. Spend a little time in cyberspace, and you'll bump into every kind of king imaginable—and plenty that you don't want to imagine.

The word "king" comes from an Old English word, *cyning*, which meant "leader of the people." About 250 years ago, people began to use it to mean "remarkably big or dominant" as in "king crab." Perhaps that's why we have so many kings now. A person can certainly be "remarkably dominant" without being a leader of the people. All he really needs is an idea and Internet access.

However, nowhere in cyberspace does anyone claim to hold even one of the titles Matthew Bridges gave to Jesus in "Crown Him with Many Crowns." In seven stanzas, Bridges crowned Jesus Lord of life, Lord of peace, Lord of love, Lord of Heaven, Lord of years, and Lord of lords. In the fifth stanza he wrote:

> Crown Him the Lord of Heaven,
> Enthroned in worlds above,
> Crown Him the King to Whom is given
> The Wondrous name of Love,
> Crown Him with many crowns,
> As thrones before Him fall;
> Crown Him, ye kings, with many crowns,
> For He is King of all.

King of All. As we slog through life, it's hard to remember that Jesus reigns over everything. He is King of Employment Opportunities and King of Financial Stability. He is sovereign over wayward children, fractured marriages and fatal illnesses. He is king in the original sense of the word—leader of the people. He leads us to victory on all these battlefields because He is the King of Kings and Lord of Lords (Revelation 19:16).

Paul wrote, "But thanks be to God, who in Christ always leads us in triumphal procession, and through us spreads the fragrance of the knowledge of him everywhere" (2 Corinthians 2:14 ESV). That's what the King of All is able to do—grant us complete success over all that threatens to defeat us. And when we sing His songs of triumph, we exalt the name of the only King who is truly worthy of the title.

119

Rest and Reflect

Psalm 47 praises the King of all the earth. Why is He worthy of praise according to the psalmist? Why are you praising Him today?

_____

_____

_____

_____

_____

_____

_____

_____

_____

_____

_____

_____

_____

_____

_____

_____

_____

_____

_____

_____

_____

_____

_____

_____

The 'Tis Now of
Loving Jesus

"My Jesus, I Love Thee" is one of my favorite hymns. The simple sincerity of its lyrics and the prayerful cadence of its melody squeeze my soul like a bear hug.

William Featherstone wrote this love letter to Jesus when he was a teenager. In stanza one he said, "For thee all the follies of sin I resign." The dictionary defines folly as "a mental weakness" or "unwise conduct." Featherstone didn't elaborate on what he considered "follies." He lived in Montreal, Canada, the largest city of British North America in the 1860s, so perhaps he meant the usual vices rampant in a metropolitan harbor—alcohol, opium, immorality, and violence.

My personal follies are different but not any less repugnant to God. When Solomon listed the six things that God "hates" in Proverbs 6,

If you love me, you will obey what I command. . . . My command is this: Love each other as I have loved you.

John 14:15, 15:12

123

he set "haughty eyes" and "a man who stirs up dissension among brothers" right beside "hands that shed innocent blood." That list makes God's definition of folly a lot more comprehensive than mine.

During the last hours Jesus spent with the disciples before He died, He wasn't lecturing them on the dangers of drunkenness or the vileness of violence; He was pleading with them to love each other. In fact, between John 13:1 and 15:19 He used the word *love* twenty-three times. And five times He repeats, "Love one another." Clearly, the folly in His disciples that concerned Jesus most was a lack of love.

124

I usually have no difficulty singing "My Jesus, I Love Thee" because I am grateful that Jesus "purchased my pardon on Calvary's tree" and wore the crown of thorns on His brow for me. It's easy to respond in love to the One who loves me unconditionally, accepts my weaknesses, forgives me quickly, and listens to every one of my prayers.

But the message He emphasized during and after the Last Supper was this: the most accurate measure of your love for Me is your love for each other. And that, quite frankly, is not easy for me. Loving those who misjudge my intentions, dismiss my concerns, and place their needs above mine—treating me as I sometimes treat them? That's nearly impossible.

Nevertheless, that's what Jesus called us to do in John 15:12. And that makes me think twice about singing "My Jesus, I Love Thee." How much do I really love Him? Enough to overlook the mistakes other people make? Enough to disregard the hurtful comments they speak? Enough to esteem others better than myself as God commands me to do in Philippians 2:3?

I don't have that kind of love. Fortunately, Jesus also said that if we stay close to Him, His love will flow through us to others because His reservoir of love is always full (John 15:4-12). That's the only way we can obey His command to love others. And the "now" of our love for Him is our willingness to allow His love to flow through us to our fellow disciples:

My Jesus, I love Thee, I know Thou art mine;
For Thee all the follies of sin I resign.
My gracious Redeemer, My Savior art Thou;
If ever I loved thee, my Jesus, 'tis now.

125

Rest and Reflect

Read Jesus' conversation with His disciples in John 13–16. If you had been there that night, what do you think He would've said to you?

127

Songs of Pain
and Praise

avid hid from King Saul in the mountains and deserts of Israel for ten years. He wrote at least twenty psalms during or about that period of his life.

David spoke to God with raw honesty. The initial tone of his psalms is often desperate and demanding: "Help, God"; "Hear, O Lord"; "Be merciful to me, O God." Psalm 13 contains a note of challenge: "How long, O LORD? Will you forget me forever?" And Psalm 22 begins with the piercing question we associate with Jesus: "My God, my God, why have you forsaken me?"

David's candor teaches us that undiluted emotion never angers God as long as it brings us to our knees before Him. The fugitive psalms are a cauldron of bubbling passions: loneliness, anger, frustration, fear, and disappointment.

Nevertheless, in each one

I will give thanks to the LORD because of his righteousness and will sing praise to the name of the LORD Most High.

Psalm 7:17

129

David journeys from perplexity to praise by shifting his focus from his circumstances to his confidence in God. In fact, David uses the words *refuge, fortress*, and *shelter* twenty-three times in these psalms.

Why should we view God as our refuge? Everything else and everyone else changes. God does not. He is the impregnable fortress. No enemy can breach the walls of His righteousness and His faithfulness. Within His gates are unlimited supplies of goodness and grace that provide the spiritual and emotional sustenance we need no matter what hardships we face.

David also counted on God's justice: "Surely there is a God who judges the earth" (58:11) and "when God restores the fortunes of his people, let Jacob rejoice and Israel be glad" (53:6). He focused on heaven, too: "Upright men will see [your] face" (11:7), and "you will fill me with joy in your presence, with eternal pleasures at your right hand" (16:11).

Because David meditated on what He knew to be true about God and His promises, he ended these psalms with praise: "The LORD redeems his servants; no one will be condemned who takes refuge in him" (34:22), and "My tongue will speak of your righteousness and of your praises all day long" (35:28).

John Newton, who wrote "Amazing Grace," also triumphed over many difficulties. One of his less familiar hymns is "How Sweet the Name of Jesus Sounds":

How sweet the name of Jesus sounds
In a believer's ear!
It soothes his sorrows, heals his wounds,
And drives away his fears.

It makes the wounded spirit whole
And calms the troubled breast;
'Tis nourishment to hungry souls,
And to the weary rest.

Jesus! Savior, Shepherd, Friend,
My Prophet, Priest, and King,
My Lord, my Life, my Way, my End,
Accept the praise I bring.

Like David's psalms, Newton's hymn teaches us what to do with our emotions: Acknowledge them honestly before God in prayer and seek refuge in the fortress of His character. In His presence alone, our mournful pleas and tearful petitions can be transformed into a testimony like David's: "I will sing to the LORD for he has been good to me"(Psalm 13:6).

Rest and Reflect

Read a psalm David wrote during the ten years he was a fugitive (eight of them are mentioned in this devotion). Pray those words back to God, making sure that you, like David, end with praise.

_____

_____

_____

_____

_____

_____

_____

_____

_____

_____

_____

_____

133

_____

_____

_____

_____

_____

_____

_____

_____

_____

_____

_____

_____

_____

Not Just a Sinner's Prayer

earing a few bars of "Just As I Am" always reminds me of the Billy Graham crusades my family watched on TV when I was a child. I'd marvel over the hundreds of people who came forward as George Beverly Shea directed the crowd to sing:

All that the Father gives me will come to me, and whoever comes to me I will never drive away.

John 6:37

Just as I am,
Without one plea,
But that thy blood
Was shed for me,
And that thou bidst me
Come to thee—
O Lamb of God,
I come, I come.

135

The lyrics of "Just As I Am" were written by an Englishwoman, Charlotte Elliot. Ira Sankey, the soloist and song leader for Dwight L. Moody, told the following story about Ms. Elliot's conversion in his autobiography*:

"At a dinner party, a preacher commented that 'he hoped she was a Christian.'" Miss Elliot was offended by his words and "replied that she would rather not discuss the question." But several weeks later, the two met again at another friend's house. Miss Elliot told the minister that she'd been thinking about his comment since their previous encounter and wanted him to explain to her how she could become a Christian. He responded, "Just come to Him as you are."

"Just As I Am" first appeared in *The Invalid's Hymn Book,* which Charlotte published in 1836, about a year after she accepted Christ as her Savior. She didn't refer specifically to her own physical limitations in the hymn; instead she focused on the mental and emotional barriers that kept her from accepting God's gift of salvation:

> Just as I am, though tossed about
> With many a conflict, many a doubt,
> Fightings and fears, within, without,
> O Lamb of God, I come, I come.

Yet she did come. She testified in the stanzas that follow that she found all she needed in Christ and that His love broke every barrier down. In the final stanza she looks forward to her heavenly home:

Just as I am, of that free love
The breadth, length, depth, and height to prove,
Here for a season, then above,
O Lamb of God, I come, I come!

I grew up thinking "Just As I Am" was a song for those who needed to accept God's gift of salvation. And it is. Its poignant lyrics have wooed thousands of people down the aisles of churches and stadiums.

But it's also a song for every Christian. Each day we come to God and confess our sins because we rely on His guarantee of forgiveness. We allow Him to "welcome" us into His arms so He can "pardon, cleanse and relieve" us of the sins that mar our fellowship with Him.

If we are to fully experience the "breadth, length, depth, and height" of His love for us, our daily prayer should be, "O Lamb of God, I come, I come."

137

---

*My Life and The Story of Gospel Hymns and of Sacred Songs and Solos. Ira D. Sankey. 1906. Philadelphia: P. W. Ziegler Co. Reprint Edition. Kessinger Publishing Rare Reprints.

Rest and Reflect

Read Jesus' words in John 6:30–40. Why did He call Himself the "true bread of heaven"? Why is that of daily importance to us?

_____

_____

_____

_____

_____

_____

_____

_____

_____

_____

_____

_____

_____

_____

_____

139

A Pet Rock
or the Eternal Rock?

*Come let us sing for joy
to the LORD;
let us shout aloud to the
Rock of our salvation.
Let us come before him
with thanksgiving and
extol him with music
and song.*
Psalm 95:1-2

Are you old enough to remember Pet Rocks— the perfect companion for kids whose parents insisted that living pets were too messy, too costly, and too time-consuming?

I had a set of those parents. I had a Pet Rock, too. At 16, I should've known that a polished stone was no substitute for what I really wanted—a dog. The Pet Rock didn't hold my interest much past the initial excitement of telling my friends I had one. And after I flipped through the pages of the *Pet Rock's Training Manual*, my "pet" took an extended nap on my dresser before its interment in the back of my bureau's bottom drawer.

I wonder how many of us treat God more as a Pet Rock than as The Eternal Rock. With enthusiasm we tell our friends that we "have" Him.

141

We display Him on our refrigerators and car bumpers dressed in witty slogans. We attach Him to our key chains and wear Him around our necks. We carry Him to church on Sundays and then return Him to our dressers where He gathers dust the rest of the week.

A relationship with that kind of God is about as meaningful as my relationship with the Pet Rock was. Consider what Moses said about The Rock he knew: "O praise the greatness of our God! He is the Rock, his works are perfect and all his ways are just. A faithful God who does no wrong, upright and just is he" (Deuteronomy 32:3-4).

142

The word translated "greatness" actually means "magnitude." Moses is telling the Israelites that God, the true God, is beyond our comprehension, both in power and in character. He is the Red Sea God. The Ten Plagues God. The Thunderous Fire on Mt. Sinai God. The Utterly Worthy of Our Worship God.

And what does The Eternal Rock say about Himself? "There is no God beside me. I put to death and I bring to life, I have wounded and I will heal, and no one can deliver out of my hand" (Deuteronomy 32:39). Infallible. Invincible. Infinitely indescribable.

No box big enough to contain Him. No manual complete enough to explain Him. No rock like this Rock. And we should never fool ourselves into thinking that anything or anyone could act as a replacement. So much more than a slogan, a convenience, or a habit—The

Eternal Rock should be the focal point of our lives.

American musician and composer George Chadwick paraphrased Psalm 95 in his hymn "Sing to the Lord, the Rock of Our Salvation." Like the psalmist, he reminds all of God's chosen people that the proper response to The Eternal Rock is grateful, humble adoration:

> Sing to the Lord, the Rock of our salvation!
> Sing to the Lord a song of joy and praise!
> Kneel in His presence, lowly in thanksgiving!
> The lofty psalm upraise!
>
> Oh, harden not your hearts, like those who wandered
> The desert forty years to Jordan's strand;
> Humble and comforted, O chosen people,
> Enter the promised land.

143

Rest and Reflect

Read Psalm 95. How has God demonstrated that He is The Eternal Rock in your life recently? Do you respond in worship to what He has done for you?

144

145

The Wondrous Love
of the Lamb

he Bible uses many symbolic names for Jesus. One that we associate closely with His redemptive work on the cross is "Lamb of God." John the Baptist first identified Jesus publicly with that name. One day as Jesus approached the Jordan River, John called out, "Behold, the Lamb of God who takes away the sin of the world" (John 1:29, NASB).

But God demonstrates his own love for us in this: While we were still sinners Christ died for us.
Romans 5:8

"Lamb of God" would have immediately signified substitution and sacrifice for the crowd who had come to hear John. Every year as the Jews prepared for Passover, they selected an unblemished lamb from their flock or purchased one in the marketplace to be used for their paschal celebration. They used the lamb's blood and its meat to commemorate the night the Angel of the Lord passed over their ancestors' homes in Egypt and spared their firstborn

147

sons (Exodus 11:1-8; 12:12-13).

But the symbolic meaning of the lamb predates the first Passover by about 500 years. Climbing Mt. Moriah toward the place of sacrifice, Isaac said to Abraham, "The wood and the fire are here, but where is the lamb for the burnt offering?" (Genesis 22:7).

I wonder how much time elapsed between Isaac's question and Abraham's response. Was Abraham's faith so strong that he quickly and confidently replied that God would provide the sacrifice? Or did the depth of his love for his son prompt him to close his eyes for a few moments as the horror of what he was about to do washed over his grief-stricken heart?

The eternal significance of Abraham's response always makes me pause: "God will provide himself a lamb" (22:8, KJV). The Hebrew word for "provide," *ra'ah*, is rich in meaning. Most often it is translated "see" as in the English expression "see to it." It suggests the duties of an overseer or a caretaker. By using *ra'ah*, Abraham acknowledged that God had chosen the sacrifice and that God was the overseer of what was about to happen.

We don't know if any of the Jews who stood by the Jordan River made the connection between the events of Genesis 22 and John the Baptist's declaration that Jesus was the Lamb of God. The idea that God would deliberately choose to sacrifice His own Son when He had spared both Isaac and the eldest sons in Egypt would have been difficult for any Jew to imagine, much less to accept as part of His perfect plan. It's difficult for us to comprehend it even though we have the Gospel records to prove it.

The unknown lyricist* of "What Wondrous Love Is This" tried to communicate his gratitude for God's unbelievable provision when he wrote these words:

What wondrous love is this, O my soul, O my soul,
What wondrous love is this, O my soul!
What wondrous love is this that caused the Lord of bliss
To bear the dreadful curse for my soul, for my soul,
To bear the dreadful curse for my soul.

What wondrous love indeed. God provided Himself as the Lamb. We may never, even in heaven, fully grasp the magnitude of that love. But we can, as the hymn suggests, express our gratitude in continual praise:

To God and to the Lamb, I will sing, I will sing;
To God and to the Lamb, I will sing.
To God and to the Lamb, Who is the Great I AM
While millions join the theme, I will sing, I will sing
While millions join the theme, I will sing.

*Note: The lyrics are sometimes attributed to American poet Alexander Means. The hymn appeared in various forms in several mid-nineteenth century hymn collections. None of those collections, however, cite Means as the lyricist. Therefore, contemporary hymnals often identify the song as an American folk hymn.

149

Denise K. Loock

Denise K. Loock

Rest and Reflect

Read Psalm 22 or Isaiah 53. Remind yourself of the magnitude of the Lamb of God's sacrifice and the depth of His love.

150

Stories of Mercy
and Grace

If you asked me to name a righteous man in Genesis, I'd say Abraham or Joseph. I wouldn't mention Lot, yet "righteous" is the adjective used in 2 Peter 2:7—God "rescued Lot, a righteous man, who was distressed by the filthy lives of lawless men."

Lot was Abraham's nephew. He made some poor choices in life. When Abraham let Lot choose where to feed his flocks, Lot "pitched his tent toward Sodom" (Genesis 13:12). Soon, he was not only living in Sodom but also sitting in the gate as a city official.

When the angels appeared in Genesis 19:1, Lot was probably a broken man, beaten down by a lifetime of unwise decisions and their consequences. But as the angels led him away from Sodom, Lot said, "I have found grace in thy sight, and thou hast magnified mercy" (Genesis 19:19, KJV).

This poor man called, and the LORD heard him; he saved him out of all his troubles.

Psalm 34:6

153

That comment indicates that he knew about God's grace and mercy, but his actions demonstrated that he didn't understand them very well.

We pair grace and mercy so often that we may begin to think they are synonyms, but they are not. Mercy is a pardon: God withholds the punishment we deserve. To be spared from the penalty of death and eternal torment in hell is mercy. Grace is a gift: God provides what we could never earn. To be adopted as God's children and given eternal life is grace.

William Newell understood the magnitude of these two gifts. As a young man he wandered far from his parents' Christian beliefs. Then Dr. R. A. Torrey gave him the opportunity to attend Moody Bible Institute in Chicago.* The more Newell learned about salvation, the more grateful he became. He expressed his gratitude in these words:

154

> Years I spent in vanity and pride,
> Caring not my Lord was crucified,
> Knowing not it was for me He died on Calvary.
>
> Mercy there was great and grace was free;
> Pardon there was multiplied to me;
> There my burdened soul found liberty at Calvary.

Lot recognized that God was gracious and merciful, but his conduct after he left Sodom indicates that he struggled with obedience (Gen. 19:15-38). On the other hand, Newell responded to God's grace with humility, gratitude, and obedience:

> Now I've given to Jesus everything,
> Now I gladly own Him as my King,
> Now my raptured soul can only sing of Calvary!

Peter identified Lot as a "righteous" man. The Greek word, *dikaios,* was used to describe both those who perceived themselves to be righteous according to their own standards and those who actually were declared righteous because of their faith in God (see Matthew 13:17 and Mark 2:17). To which group did Lot belong? We don't know. The more relevant question is, to which group do we belong?

The more completely we understand grace and mercy, the more grateful and obedient we will become. Like Newell, we will respond to The God of All Grace and Mercy with humble hearts, and we'll gladly serve Him as our King.

---

*Biographical information on Newell gleaned from *Al Smith's Treasury of Hymn Histories*. Special Library Edition. Heritage Music Distributors, Inc. 1982.

Rest and Reflect

Paul explained what our response to God's mercy and grace should be in Romans 6:11-14. How can you be an "instrument of righteousness" today?

_____

_____

_____

_____

_____

_____

_____

_____

_____

_____

_____

_____

_____

_____

_____

_____

_____

_____

_____

_____

_____

Resurrection Sunday

. . . Death has been swallowed up in victory.
1 Corinthians 15:54

very year as Easter approaches, the debate about calling it "Easter" or "Resurrection Sunday" arises in the Christian community. The word "Easter" derived from an Old English word, *Easterdæg*, and referred to a festival dedicated to Austron, a goddess of fertility and spring. The poet Bede (673-735AD) said that Anglo-Saxon Christians adapted Austron's name and many of the practices associated with her festival for their celebration of Christ's resurrection.* Therefore, many contemporary Christians, aware of the pagan roots of "Easter," prefer to use "Resurrection Sunday."

Because my father was a well-known Bible teacher and conference speaker, people often asked him about the "Easter" issue. He'd usually respond with slightly raised eyebrows and an enigmatic

159

grin. Then he'd growl, "Every Sunday is Resurrection Sunday."

His point, of course, was that every Sunday commemorates Jesus' resurrection. That's the reason the apostles shifted their day of worship from Saturday to Sunday. Throughout the Old Testament, Jews worshiped on the seventh day of the week, the Sabbath, because God rested from the work of creation on that day (Ex. 20:8-11). The early church, however, met on the first day of the week—a constant reminder that the New Covenant established by the Risen Christ had replaced the Old Covenant instituted by the Mosaic Law (see Acts 20:7, 1 Cor. 16:2).

160

Jesus' resurrection is the cornerstone of the New Covenant. As Paul told the Corinthians, "If Christ has not been raised, our preaching is useless and so is your faith" (1 Cor. 15:12). And just a few verses later he said, "If Christ has not been raised, your faith is futile; you are still in your sins" (v. 17). The Greek word translated "useless" in verse 12 and "futile" in verse 17 means "empty, to no purpose, of no effect." Christ's resurrection proved that He had power over death. Without that proof, we'd have no viable reason to expect either victory over sin on earth or eternal life in heaven.

That reminds me of another point Dad used to make. Why do we relegate the celebration of the Resurrection to one day a year? Not only is every Sunday Resurrection Sunday, but also every day is Resurrection Day for those of us who have accepted God's gift of salvation.

Each day that we wake up, we reap the benefits of His resurrection. Each time we resist a temptation, we access the power of His resurrection. Each time we choose to praise God instead of yielding to discouragement or anger, we experience the freedom that Jesus' resurrection provided for us.

Maybe Charles Wesley wanted to emphasize the daily-ness of resurrection power when he wrote the following stanzas of "Christ the Lord Is Risen Today":

Soar we now where Christ hath led, Alleluia!
Following our exalted Head, Alleluia!
Made like Him, like Him we rise, Alleluia!
Ours the cross, the grave, the skies, Alleluia!

King of glory, Soul of bliss, Alleluia!
Everlasting life is this, Alleluia!
Thee to know, Thy power to prove, Alleluia!
Thus to sing and thus to love, Alleluia!

The power to "soar" each day and to "prove" that Christ delivered us from the power of sin is the evidence that "death has been swallowed up in victory." Through the resurrection of our Lord and Savior, God gives each of us the ability to live a life that brings Him glory. That's reason enough to declare every day Resurrection Day.

---

http://www.etymonline.com/index.php?term=Easter&allowed_in_frame=0

Rest and Reflect

Read 1 Corinthians 15, Paul's soaring commentary on the importance of the resurrection. What can resurrection victory empower you to do today?

163

Making God Look Good

In the corner of the living room of my childhood home stood a stereo console. On it my mom played a stack of Christian records all day long. I don't remember who the vocalist was, but one song I heard often was "Jesus Is All the World to Me":

. . .so now also Christ shall be magnified in my body, whether it be by life, or by death.
Philippians 1:20 (KJV)

Jesus is all the world to me,
My life, my joy, my all;
He is my strength
From day to day,
Without Him I would fall.
When I am sad,
To Him I go,
No other one
Can cheer me so;
When I am sad,
He makes me glad,
He's my friend.

American composer and publisher William Thompson wrote the lyrics to that gospel song. The devotion to Christ conveyed in his words reminds

165

me of Paul's words in Philippians 1:21—"For to me, to live is Christ and to die is gain."

Paul was a prisoner in Rome when he wrote Philippians. He didn't know whether his death was imminent or not. According to verse 23, Paul wanted to "depart and be with Christ which [he considered] better by far." Yet he realized that what he desired and what God desired could be two different things—which is why he said what he did in verse 21.

Paul explained what he meant by "to me to live is Christ" in verse 20—whether he lived or died he wanted Christ to be "exalted in [his] body." The Greek word for "magnified" (KJV) or "exalted" (NIV) means "made conspicuous." In other words, whatever displayed God's glory most is what Paul desired most. Therefore, he accepted that his desire to be in heaven might be superseded by God's desire that he remain on earth to encourage and teach others—"for your progress and joy in the faith" (vv.24-26).

When I was young, Philippians 1:21 was a tough verse for me to digest because I wanted to do so many things before I went to heaven—get married, pursue a teaching career, have kids, and travel in Europe. At that time, I didn't view dying as "gain" – which literally means "to my advantage." Now that I'm older my perspective has changed. On many days I do see dying as an advantage. Freedom from disappointments and trials looks pretty good to me sometimes.

But Paul's point in this passage is that living, or dying, for Christ isn't about what we want or don't want. It's about what displays God's glory most—what "makes God look good."*

That's what "Jesus is all the world to me" really means—the goal of my life, Jesus, is to make You look good. Will that be through physical suffering or financial hardship? Will it be through imprisonment? Paul experienced all those things.

When he dictated his letter to the Philippians Paul said, " Pray for me. Pray that I will have sufficient courage to make God look good even in my present circumstances." (1:20, paraphrase mine). If Jesus really is "all the world" to us, then that will be our prayer as well.

167

*keynote speaker Kathy Benjamin's phrase, EFCA Eastern District Women's Retreat, Camp Spofford, New Hampshire. September 17, 2011.

Rest and Reflect

Read 2 Corinthians 4:8-18. What hardships did Paul suffer for Christ's sake? What was his attitude about them? What is your response to your hardships?

_____

_____

_____

_____

_____

_____

_____

_____

_____

_____

_____

_____

_____

_____

_____

_____

_____

_____

169

What's So Great about God's Greatness?

Great is the Lord, and greatly to be praised, and his greatness is unsearchable.

Psalm 145:3

The word *great* has lost its greatness. Overuse and misuse have toppled it.

Dethroned and disgraced, it's been relegated to the Most Unwanted Adjectives posters taped to the walls of English classrooms and editorial offices across the country.

Dictionary.com lists twenty-four" definitions and provides hundreds of synonyms for this once majestic and mighty adjective. But its uses have become so diverse and diluted, that it might as well ask *a, an,* and *the* if it can be an article.

For example, the Great Barrier Reef and the Great Wall of China are so named because of their size. Dickens titled one of his novels *Great Expectations* because the main character had lofty but unreachable aspirations. Comedic actor Jackie Gleason was crowned "The Great One" for his ability to dominate

171

a stage and his appetite for a luxurious lifestyle; boxer Muhammed Ali acquired Gleason's title because of his athletic dexterity and inflated ego.

So when we sing songs like "How Great Thou Art," what exactly do we mean? God's big? Unreachable? Talented? Dominating? That hymn's lyrics, translated into English by Stuart Hines, praise God's creative genius and His redemptive grace. But is that the extent of God's greatness?

The Hebrew word for *great* comes from a root word that means "to twist together." It refers to the strength of a rope composed of many threads twisted together—the more threads, the stronger the rope.

The longer I reflected on this concept of greatness, the more appropriate it seemed as a description of God. A powerful God is good. A loving God is good. Twist power and love together, and you begin to understand His greatness. As I mentally entwined the threads of God's character, the splendor of His greatness increased: justice and forgiveness, righteousness and compassion, strength and tenderness.

No wonder the psalmist exclaimed, "His greatness is unsearchable." The greatness of God extends way beyond immensity, intensity, or diversity. It's bound up in the infinite complexity of His nature.

The word translated "unsearchable" means "past finding out." In other words, no amount of investigation will ever make the subject under consideration comprehendible. So add the thread of incomprehensibility to God's character. (I can barely pronounce the word, much less understand it.)

Remember what the apostle John said at the end of his gospel? "Jesus did many other things as well. If every one of them were written down, I suppose that even the whole world would not have room for the books that would be written" (21:25). If that's how John felt after spending three years with one person of the Godhead confined in a human body, imagine how much more "unsearchable" the Triune Godhead is.

No one knows who wrote the lyrics to "I Will Extol Thee, O My God," a paraphrase of Psalm 145. The hymn reminds us of what the proper response to God's greatness should be: the gratitude that swells in our hearts should compel us to dwell on His majesty and tell others of all His grand and glorious works:

173

I will extol Thee, O my God,
And praise Thee, O my King;
Yea, every day and evermore
Thy praises will I sing.
Great is the Lord, our mighty God,
And greatly to be praised.
His greatness is unsearchable,
Above all glory raised.

Each generation to the next
Shall testimony bear,
And to Thy praise, from age to age,
Thy wondrous acts declare;
Upon Thy glorious majesty
And honor will I dwell.
And all Thy grand and glorious works
And all Thy greatness tell.

The more we meditate on the multi-faceted wonders of God's greatness, the more awestruck we'll be. And like the biblical writers and hymnists, we'll be quick to declare His wondrous acts to others.

Rest and Reflect

Read Psalm 145. What manifestations of God's greatness have been evident in your life lately? Have you told anyone about those "glorious works"?

In Clouds of Great Power and Glory

At that time men will see the Son of Man coming in clouds with great power and glory.
Mark 13:26

When I visited my parents in Hudson, Florida, with my husband and children, we often took a 15-minute after-dinner drive to watch the sun set over the Gulf of Mexico.

The pinks, blues, purples, and golds the setting sun painted were sometimes vivid, sometimes pastel. Often the clouds puffed up like bags of microwave popcorn; on other nights they stretched across the horizon like frayed edges of a worn beach towel.

When the sun displayed its tail feathers like a peacock, I'd wonder, *Is this what the sky will look like on the day Christ returns? Will the sun's rays shoot upward like golden heralds announcing His arrival?*

Jesus was speaking only to His disciples in Mark 13 when He announced that He would return in clouds of glory and power. Later, at His trial He

177

also told the Sanhedrin, "You will see the Son of Man sitting at the right hand of the Mighty One and coming on the clouds of heaven" (Matthew 26:64).

According to Thayer's Lexicon, the Greek word translated "clouds" in these verses specifically refers to the supernatural cloud of God's presence that led the Israelites after they left Egypt. Exodus 13:21 says, "By day the LORD went ahead of them in a pillar of cloud, to guide them on their way; and by night in a pillar of fire to give them light."

The Cloud of God's Presence was like no other cloud. First of all, it was so large that two million Israelites could see it. The word *pillar*, sometimes translated "column," referred to the cloud's height. According to the Gesenius Lexicon, high mountains were called "the pillars of heaven" in Moses' time, so imagine Mount Everest hovering above the Israelites as they journeyed through the wilderness.

Exodus 14:20 provides another unique detail about the Cloud of God's Presence. On the night God parted the Red Sea, "the cloud brought darkness to the [Egyptians] and light to the [Israelites]." Later, when God descended to Mount Sinai, we get a similar image of His presence providing both darkness and light. In Deuteronomy 4:11 Moses said that the mountain "blazed with fire to the very heavens, with black clouds and deep darkness."

These descriptions make it clear that when Jesus

returns in clouds of glory, no one will mistake His arrival for a particularly impressive sunset. The reaction will probably be more like the Israelites' at Sinai: "Everyone in the camp trembled" (Exodus 19:16). And they only saw the manifestation of God's presence, not God Himself.

William M. Runyan was a Methodist pastor, an editor, and a hymn writer. In "Again He'll Come" he reflected on the day when "The Son of God shall come in glory splendid":

> Again, again, the nations shall behold Him!
> Again, again, enrobed in majesty;
> In clouds of glory every eye shall see Him,
> Again, again, the King of Glory see!

179

Will the return of the King of Glory bring the darkness of judgment or the light of deliverance? That depends. Will those who witness Jesus' return be welcoming a Long-Awaited Savior or facing a Long-Suffering Judge?

Rest and Reflect

Read Exodus 20:18-21. Why do you think the people responded so differently to the LORD's presence than Moses did? How would you have responded?

Denise K. Loock

Loving Clara
Cloudburst

... Having loved his own who were in the world, he loved them to the end.

John 13:1 NASB

'm not very loveable sometimes. Just ask my husband. Or my kids. I can be cranky, judgmental, and downright cantankerous. I screech. I whine. I rant. Many people think of me as Suzy Sunshine. But if they lived with me 24/7, they'd discover that Clara Cloudburst lives inside me, too.

The disciples weren't very loveable either. That's why John 13:1 is such a comforting verse. John had lived with Jesus 24/7 for three years. He'd witnessed a panorama of emotions among his fellow disciples— their fear, their self-absorption, their unbelief. And he'd seen how Jesus loved them anyway.

When John wrote his gospel, he remembered the steadfastness of his Savior's love. And he realized that every moment of every day he'd spent with Jesus was leading to the ultimate display of His

183

love—His atoning sacrifice on the cross.

John also remembered how obtuse he and all of his peers had been. They were weak and willful, foolish and forgetful. How many times did Jesus rebuke them with "O you of little faith"? How many times did He reassure them with "Don't be afraid"?

On the night Jesus was betrayed, He admonished Philip, "Don't you know me even after I have been among you such a long time?" (John 14:9). The disciples had listened to Jesus' words of life and observed His life of light for "three years, but they still lived" in ignorance and walked in darkness.

Sometimes we post-resurrection Christians criticize the disciples for their lack of faith and understanding. We marvel, "Jesus was right with them. How could they not believe?" Well, Jesus lives *within* us. How can we not believe? How can we not trust the One who loves us "to the end"?

Phillip Bliss was a prolific American hymn writer. He understood the Clara Cloudburst syndrome very well. He wrote these words in "Jesus Loves Even Me":

I am so glad that my Father in heaven
Tells of His love in the Book He has given:
Wonderful things in the Bible I see—
This is the dearest that Jesus loves me.

Though I forget Him and wander away,
Still Jesus loves me wherever I stray:
Back to His dear loving arms I would flee,
O, what a wonder that Jesus loves me.

I am so glad that Jesus loves me,
Jesus loves me, Jesus loves me;
I am so glad that Jesus loves me,
Jesus loves even me.

Jesus told the disciples, "Just as the Father has loved me, I have also loved you; abide in my love" (John 15:9 NASB). If we rest in the steadfastness of His love we will know, even on Clara Cloudburst days, that nothing can ever separate us from the security of His everlasting devotion. "O, what a wonder that Jesus loves me."

Rest and Reflect

Soak your soul in the soothing waters of God's love today by meditating on Jesus' promises in John 15:1–14.

The Name of the LORD Jesus Christ

ncluded in the dramatic Genesis narrative of the Creation, the Fall, and the Flood is a significant statement that's easy to miss—"at that time men began to call on the name of the LORD" (4:26).

Why is that simple sentence so important? It signifies the beginning of the organized worship of God's people and their desire to set themselves apart as worshipers of Jehovah, the one true God. According to the Gesenius Lexicon, "to call on the name of the LORD [is] to celebrate, to praise his name, and to ask for his aid."

Throughout Old Testament times, a line was drawn between those who knew the LORD and called upon His name, and those who did not know Him and turned to idols. For example, Moses told Pharaoh repeatedly that God was using the severity of the

Everyone who calls upon the name of the LORD will be saved.
Romans 10:13

189

plagues to make His name known among the Egyptians, among the Israelites who had forsaken Him, and among all the nations of the world (see Exodus 7:5, 6:7, 9:14-15). David proclaimed that truth in the Valley of Elah just before he killed Goliath (1 Samuel 17:46). Elijah demonstrated it on Mount Carmel (1 Kings 18:37). And Nebuchadnezzar learned it after he spent seven years eating grass (Daniel 4:34-35).

In the Old Testament, those who called on the name of the LORD, *Jehovah*, and worshiped Him were saved. But after the death and resurrection of Jesus, it was no longer enough to bring sacrifices to *Jehovah* for the forgiveness of sin. Christ's sacrificial death on the cross mandated that every person call on His name to be saved.

190

When Peter, the uneducated fisherman, stood before the most learned religious people of his era in Acts 4, he boldly proclaimed, "It is by the name of Jesus Christ of Nazareth . . . that this man stands before you healed . . . Salvation is found in no one else [other than Jesus]" (v. 10-12). Throughout the Book of Acts the apostles preached forgiveness of sins through "the name of Jesus" (5:40, 9:27-29, 10:48).

Many people today are willing to call upon an amorphous god for a variety of reasons. But only if they call upon the name of the LORD Jesus Christ will their sins be forgiven, and only then will they be given the gift of eternal life.

Caroline Maria Noel, an Englishwoman who was an invalid for most of her life, wrote the lyrics to "At the Name of Jesus." This hymn is an eloquent reflection on the power of Jesus' name:

At the Name of Jesus, every knee shall bow,
Every tongue confess Him King of glory now;
'Tis the Father's pleasure we should call Him Lord,
Who from the beginning was the mighty Word.

Name Him, brothers, name Him, with love strong as death
But with awe and wonder, and with bated breath!
He is God the Savior, He is Christ the Lord,
Ever to be worshipped, trusted and adored.

191

Once we have accepted God's gift of salvation, what should the matchless name of Jesus motivate us to do? Noel answered that question as well:

In your hearts enthrone Him; there let Him subdue
All that is not holy, all that is not true;
Crown Him as your Captain in temptation's hour;
Let His will enfold you in its light and power.

Rest and Reflect

Read Deuteronomy 32:1-4. How did Moses proclaim the name of the LORD throughout his life? How can you proclaim His name today? Consider what Paul says in Colossians 3:17.

192

In Life
and In Death

Be strong and courageous . . . for the LORD your God goes with you. He will never leave you or forsake you.
Deuteronomy 31:6

I sang a lot of hymns the week my mother died. Not in a choir. Or even in the shower. My sister and I sang them at our mother's bedside as her earthly sojourn ended.

We sang the songs we knew she loved like "In the Garden" and "Through It All." We soothed our aching hearts with "It Is Well with My Soul" and "Jesus, I Am Resting, Resting." We gave her glimpses of her new home with "When the Roll Is Called Up Yonder" and "Face to Face."

But the hymn that took up residence in my mind and in my heart that week was Henry F. Lyte's "Abide with Me." When Lyte wrote those lyrics, he knew he was dying of tuberculosis. Yet, as his words indicate, he did not allow sorrow to overwhelm him:

195

I fear no foe, with Thee at hand to bless;
Ills have no weight and tears no bitterness;
Where is death's sting? Where, grave, thy victory?
I triumph still if Thou abide with me.

I'll never know until I get to heaven whether Mom knew how close to death she was. She must have at least known that something was very amiss as the massive infection spread through her jaw, throat, and into her brain. I do know that she longed for heaven and for freedom from the body that had stolen her independence and clarity of thought.

Mom never did sing very well. And after her salivary gland was removed in 2001 due to squamous carcinoma cancer, she wasn't able to sing at all. But as I sang "Abide with Me" to her, I know her heart was singing, especially this stanza:

Hold Thou Thy cross before my closing eyes;
Shine through the gloom and point me to the skies;
Heaven's morning breaks
And earth's vain shadows flee;
In life, in death, O Lord, abide with me.

I have no doubt that "in death" the Lord was abiding with Mom. I didn't see the angels carry Mom to Glory, but I know they did. And I know that millions of the heavenly hosts lined the golden streets and applauded

196

as her guardian angels guided her through heaven's gates.

I also know that the Lord is abiding with me and all my family members as we continue life on earth without Mom. As I write these words, the following lyrics steady my hands and my heart:

Change and decay in all around I see;
O Thou who changest not, abide with me.

No matter what roller coaster ride we're on, the safety bar of God's character keeps us secure. Grab hold of it and don't let go. Though our hands tremble and our hearts pound, our souls can rest in the "peace that transcends all understanding" (Philippians 4:7). Our Savior sits beside us, His hands securely covering ours.

197

Denise K. Loock

Rest and Reflect

Read Isaiah's words of comfort and hope in Isaiah 25:4-9. Can you sing the song of thanksgiving he sings in Isaiah 26:1-4?

198

Acknowledgments

Thanks to my husband and children
who continue to fend for themselves
as I sit at the computer hour after hour.
Without their forbearance and self-sufficiency,
I'd probably never finish a manuscript.

Thanks to Mark Hahn and the MEFC sanctuary choir
for their continued encouragement, feedback, and support
for the Take Note devotions each week.

Thanks to my manuscript readers—
Dianne, Connie, Fran, and Lucy.
Your editing, proofreading, and insights are invaluable.

Thanks, Phyllis.
Your eagle eye for error keeps me humble.

Song Index

Denise K. Loock